READING/WRITING
COMPANION

Mc
Graw
Hill
Education

Cover: Nathan Love, Erwin Madrid

mheducation.com/prek-12

Send all inquiries to:
McGraw-Hill Education
Two Penn Plaza
New York, NY 10121

ISBN: 978-0-07-901818-2
MHID: 0-07-901818-1

Printed in the United States of America.

5 6 7 8 9 LMN 23 22 21   B

Welcome to Wonders!

Read exciting **Literature**, **Science**, and **Social Studies** texts!

★ LEARN about the world around you!

★ THINK, SPEAK, and WRITE about genres!

★ COLLABORATE in discussion and inquiry!

★ EXPRESS yourself!

my.mheducation.com

Use your student login to read core texts, practice grammar and spelling, explore research projects and more!

GENRE STUDY **1 BIOGRAPHY**

SOCIAL STUDIES

 Digital Tools Find this eBook and other resources at **my.mheducation.com**

GENRE STUDY 2 REALISTIC FICTION

SOCIAL STUDIES

GENRE STUDY **3 PERSUASIVE ARTICLE**

WRAP UP THE UNIT

Talk About It

U.S. COAST GUARD AIRRANGER

COLLABORATE

A hero is someone who is looked up to by others because of his or her achievements and courage. A rescue worker is a hero to many people.

Discuss with a partner what is happening in the photo. Then talk about people you think are heroes. Write your ideas in the chart.

SOCIAL STUDIES

Hero	What Makes Them a Hero

TAKE NOTES

Asking questions before reading helps you figure out what you want to learn, or your purpose for reading. Write your question here.

_____

_____

_____

_____

As you read, make note of:

Interesting Words _____

_____

_____

Key Details _____

_____

_____

César Chávez

Essential Question

What do heroes do?

Read about a man who took action to improve the lives of others.

Who are your **heroes?** For many farm workers, César Chávez is a hero. He is the brave man who spent his life helping them.

Childhood

César Chávez was born in Arizona. His parents taught him about learning, hard work, and respect.

César worked on the family farm as a young boy. He helped care for the farm animals. His mother and grandmother taught César about caring. Many people came to their door asking for food, and his kind family always shared.

César had a strong **interest** in education. This desire to learn was sometimes hard on him. Spanish was his first language, but he needed to learn and **study** English. At school, he was punished for speaking Spanish.

His mother taught César to find peaceful ways to solve problems. These lessons helped him **succeed** later in life. He would win struggles without fighting.

Susan Swan

FIND TEXT EVIDENCE

Read
Paragraphs 2–3
Summarize
Circle what César Chávez's family taught him about. Summarize how he learned about caring for others.

_____

_____

_____

Paragraph 5
Sequence
Draw a box around what César's mother taught him. **Underline** how this helped him succeed later in life.

Reread
Author's Craft

How does the author get you interested in the biography in the first paragraph?

FIND TEXT EVIDENCE

Read

Paragraph 1-2

Boldprint and Timeline

Underline what the drought caused. **Circle** two reasons why the family moved. **Circle** this event on the timeline.

Paragraph 3

Summarize

Draw a box around what the family discovered in California. Summarize details that tell about what they discovered.

_____

_____

_____

Reread

Author's Craft

How does the timeline help you understand César's work and accomplishments?

Hard Times

When César was ten, it did not rain for a long time. This **drought** caused the plants on the farm to die. Without **crops** to sell, César's family couldn't afford to keep the farm.

Then César's family moved to California where there was no drought. His family traveled from farm to farm and worked the crops.

César and his family would quickly **discover** that migrant farm workers had difficult lives. Their **challenging** jobs forced them to work long hours for little money. The workers bent over all day tending the crops. The work they had to **perform** made their backs hurt and their fingers bleed. If workers complained, farm owners fired them.

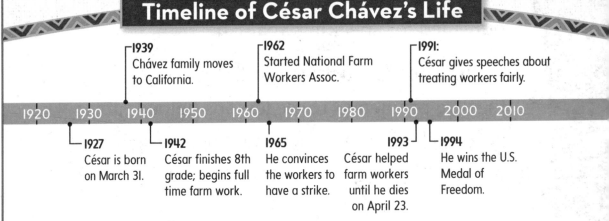

Timeline of César Chávez's Life

1939
Chávez family moves to California.

1962
Started National Farm Workers Assoc.

1991:
César gives speeches about treating workers fairly.

1920   1930   1940   1950   1960   1970   1980   1990   2000   2010

1927
César is born on March 31.

1942
César finishes 8th grade; begins full time farm work.

1965
He convinces the workers to have a strike.

1993
César helped farm workers until he dies on April 23.

1994
He wins the U.S. Medal of Freedom.

Changing Lives

César knew the migrant workers were not treated fairly so he decided to take action. He told the migrant workers he had a plan.

It was time for grapes to be harvested, or picked. César told the workers to stop working. This was called a **strike**. The grapes began to rot. With no grapes to sell, the landowners lost money. Finally, the owners talked to César. They promised better pay. After that, the workers began picking the crops again.

César Chávez worked for the rest of his life to improve farm workers' lives. Would you **agree** that he is a hero?

Summarize

Use details in the text and the timeline to summarize the events in "César Chávez" in order.

Susan Swan

FIND TEXT EVIDENCE

Read

Paragraph 2

Synonyms

Draw a box around a synonym for *harvested*. When did César tell workers to stop working?

_____

_____

_____

Sequence

Underline what happened when the landowners lost money. **Circle** what happened after that.

Reread

Author's Craft

Why does the author ask a question at the conclusion, or end, of the biography?

Vocabulary

**Talk with a partner about each word.
Then answer the questions.**

agree

My friend and I **agree** to share the ball.

What is something you and a friend agree about?

_____

_____

challenging

This math problem is **challenging** to me.

Tell about something that is challenging for you
to do.

_____

_____

discover

I **discover** fun books to read at school.

What are some things you want to discover?

_____

_____

_____

heroes

Firefighters are **heroes** that help others.

What other people are heroes?

_____

_____

interest

Adam has an **interest** in music.

Tell about an interest of yours.

_____

_____

Build Your Word List On page 5,
find three different words that
have the root word *work*. Use a word
web to write the words you found.

perform

My class likes to **perform** songs at school.

Tell about a time you saw someone perform.

_____

_____

study

I like to **study** the planets.

What do you like to study?

_____

_____

succeed

I hope I **succeed** in winning the game.

What do you do if you do not succeed at something at first?

_____

_____

Synonyms

Synonyms are words that have almost the same meaning. *Mad* and *angry* are synonyms. A synonym can be a clue to the meaning of a difficult word.

FIND TEXT EVIDENCE

On page 3 of "César Chávez," I read the word caring. *In the last sentence of the same paragraph, I read the word* kind. Caring *and* kind *are synonyms.*

His mother and grandmother taught César about caring. Many people came to their door asking for food, and his kind family always shared.

 Your Turn Find a synonym for the word below.

problems, page 3 _____

Write your own sentence using one pair of synonyms.

Susan Swan

Summarize

Summarizing is using your own words to tell the most important details. This can help you remember information.

🔍 **FIND TEXT EVIDENCE**
After reading page 5 of "César Chávez," I can summarize what César did to help farm workers.

Page 5

It was time for the grapes to be harvested, or picked. César told the workers to stop working. This was called a **strike**. The grapes began to rot. With no grapes to sell, the landowners lost money. Finally, the owners talked to César. They promised better pay. After that, the workers began picking the crops again.

I read that César talked to other farm workers and they had a strike. When the owners promised better pay, the strike ended.

Your Turn Summarize the section "Childhood" on page 3.

_____

_____

_____

Bold Print and Timeline

"César Chávez" is a biography. It is a true story of a person's life that is written by another person. The author uses text features, such as words in bold print and a timeline.

 FIND TEXT EVIDENCE

I can tell that "César Chávez" is a biography because it tells about the life of César Chávez. Another clue is that it has a timeline of his life and important words in bold print.

Readers to Writers

Use a timeline to show the order of important events in a biography. Label the years of the events to show when they took place during a person's life.

Page 4

Hard Times

When César was ten, it did not rain for a long time. This **drought** caused the plants on the farm to die. Without **crops** to sell, César's family couldn't afford to keep the farm.

Then César's family moved to California where there was no drought. His family traveled from farm to farm and worked the crops.

César and his family would quickly **discover** that migrant farm workers had difficult lives. Their **challenging** jobs forced them to work long hours for little money. The workers bent over all day tending the crops. The work they had to **perform** made their backs hurt and their fingers bleed. If workers complained, farm owners fired them.

Timeline of César Chávez's Life

| 1927 | 1939 | 1942 | 1962 | 1965 | 1993 | 1994 | 1991 |

- 1939 Chávez family moves to California.
- 1962 Started National Farm Workers Assoc.
- 1991 César gives speeches about treating workers fairly.
- 1927 César is born on March 31.
- 1942 César finishes 8th grade; begins full time farm work.
- 1965 He convinces the workers to have a strike.
- 1993 César helped farm workers until he dies on April 23.
- 1994 He wins the U.S. Medal of Freedom.

1920 1930 1940 1950 1960 1970 1980 1990 2000 2010

Bold print shows words that are important to understand the topic.

A **timeline** shows dates of events in the order that they happened.

 Your Turn How does the author use the timeline to add details to the biography?

Sequence

The sequence tells the order of ideas in a text. We can use the words *first*, *next*, *then*, and *last* to tell the order of what happens.

FIND TEXT EVIDENCE

As I read "César Chávez," I think about how the ideas and information are organized in the text. They tell the sequence of events in César's life.

First
César Chávez was born on a farm in Arizona.

 Your Turn Reread "César Chávez." Fill in the graphic organizer to help you identify the sequence of important events.

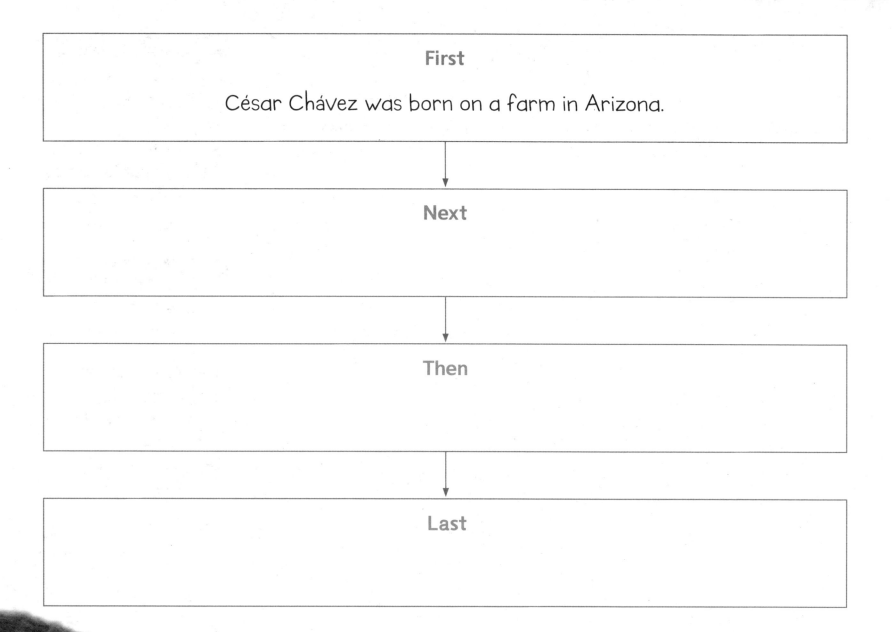

First

César Chávez was born on a farm in Arizona.

Next

Then

Last

Respond to Reading

COLLABORATE

Talk about the prompt below. Think about the text features the author uses. Use your notes and graphic organizer.

Explain why César Chávez is a hero. What text features helped you understand more about his life?

_____

_____

_____

_____

_____

_____

_____

Paraphrase

To **paraphrase** means to use your own words to retell what someone has written. When you take notes from a source, paraphrasing will help you understand the information.

Read the text below. Then write the same information using your own words.

> Author of the Declaration of Independence in 1776, Thomas Jefferson led our nation as President from 1801 to 1809.

_____

_____

_____

American Hero Poster With a partner, research the life of an American hero, such as Paul Revere, Amelia Earhart, or Sojourner Truth. Then create a poster with information that tells why this person is important in American history.

My American hero is _____

As you research, remember to paraphrase the most important information to include in your poster.

Look away from a source when you take notes. This will help you write down ideas in your own words.

Brave Bessie

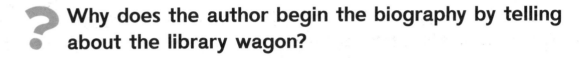 **Why does the author begin the biography by telling about the library wagon?**

Literature Anthology: pages 390–401

Talk About It Reread page 391. Discuss how Bessie feels about the books from the library wagon.

Cite Text Evidence Write details that tell why the library wagon was important to Bessie. Then write how the details help you understand what Bessie did later.

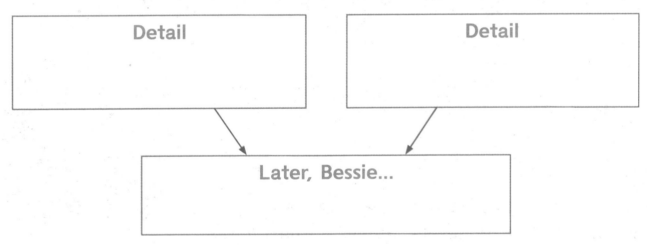

Detail	Detail

Later, Bessie...

Write The author begins by telling about the library

wagon because _____

_____

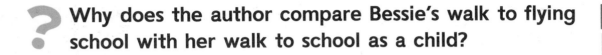
? **Why does the author compare Bessie's walk to flying school with her walk to school as a child?**

Talk About It Reread paragraph 1 on page 392 and paragraph 3 on page 396. What did Bessie do each day?

Text Evidence Take notes on the paragraphs. Then tell what the details both show.

In Texas, Bessie...	These details both show...
In France, Bessie...	

Write The author compares Bessie's two walks to _____

_____

_____

Quick Tip

Use these sentence starters to help you explain why Besssie walked so far.

Bessie knew school was...

Bessie had to walk...

Bessie practiced...

Combine Information

Think about what Bessie had needed to do to get to France and what she did in France. What do these details all show?

? **How does the timeline help you to understand what Bessie accomplished, or achieved?**

Talk About It Reread the timeline on page 398. Talk about the important events that it shows.

Cite Text Evidence Write key details from the selection for three of Bessie's accomplishments on the timeline.

Quick Tip

The author described Bessie's life in the order that events happened. Use the timeline to identify what you have learned about Bessie and why she is a hero to people.

Year	Event

Write The timeline helps me understand Bessie's

accomplishments because _____

_____

_____

Respond to Reading

Discuss the prompt below with your partner. Think about what you know about heroes and have learned about Bessie Coleman. Use your notes to help you.

How does the author use Bessie's story to show what it means to be a hero?

_____

_____

_____

_____

_____

_____

_____

The Prince's Frog

Literature Anthology:
pages 402-405

The Queen noticed her son's disappointment. "Take good care of your royal pet," she told him. "Make sure that your frog has everything a frog needs to be healthy and happy." Peter felt glum, but he did as he was told. He put the frog in a dish of water. He captured flies and fed his pet. *Snap, gulp!* The frog's sticky tongue darted out and swallowed hungrily. "Yuck!" Peter thought.

Reread the text. **Underline** what the Queen tells her son to do. **Circle** words that describe how Peter feels.

Draw a box around the description of the frog eating. Why does Peter think "Yuck!" when he watches the frog?

_____

_____

_____

COLLABORATE

How does the author help you understand that it is difficult for Peter to take care of his new pet frog?

For three days, the Queen watched as Peter's interest in the frog grew. She was happy to see her son and his pet splash and laugh in the royal pool. Peter always made sure the frog was safe and had everything a frog needs to be healthy and happy. The Queen was pleased to see her son take good care of his pet.

On the third night, the frog told the prince, "I feel lucky to be your pet."

Peter felt lucky, too. A prince could never wish for a better pet then his friendly frog. He kissed the frog on its slimy head. "I will always take care of you, my friend."

Reread paragraph 1. **Underline** why the Queen is happy. What details in the text and illustration show Peter is having fun with his pet?

_____

_____

_____

Circle what Peter does for his pet. **Draw a box** around what the Queen is pleased to see.

COLLABORATE

Discuss how the author describes the Queen's feelings as a way to tell you about Peter.

? **How does the author help you understand how Peter's feelings change in the story?**

Talk About It Reread pages 18 and 19. Talk about details
COLLABORATE that show how Peter feels about his pet.

Cite Text Evidence Write details about the character Peter.
Then tell how his feelings change in the story.

Quick Tip

Story characters may change as they learn an important lesson. Peter's feelings about his pet frog change in the story. Think about what he has learned by the end.

Details	How Peter Changes

Write The author helps me understand how _____

_____

_____

Point of View

The narrator of "The Prince's Frog" is *not* a character. The fairy tale is told from the third-person point of view. The narrator uses pronouns such as *he* or *she* to show the actions, thoughts, and feelings of the characters.

FIND TEXT EVIDENCE

On page 18, the pronouns *her* and *she* refer to, or tell about, the Queen. The narrator shows what the Queen does and says from the third-person point of view.

> The Queen noticed her son's disappointment. "Take good care of your royal pet," she told him.

Your Turn Look back at page 19. What pronouns refer to

Peter from the third-person point of view? _____

Identify when the narrator uses the third-person point of view to describe the feelings of the Queen and Peter.

_____

_____

_____

Quick Tip

Authors can use the third-person point of view to tell what different characters think or feel about events in a story.

? **What have you learned about what heroes do from the selections and the statue of Paul Revere?**

Talk About It Look at the photograph and read the caption. Talk with a partner about what you know about Paul Revere. Why do you think he is a hero?

Cite Text Evidence **Circle** the detail in the caption that tells why the statue has been built. **Underline** why people think Paul Revere is a hero.

Write The selections I read and this photograph

help me understand that heroes are _____

_____

_____

_____

_____

_____

_____

Use the sentence starters to discuss what heroes do.

César worked to...

Bessie Coleman wanted to...

Peter became a hero because...

Paul Revere...

The sculpture honors Paul Revere's famous Midnight Ride. He risked his life to help protect the safety of others.

Present Your Work

COLLABORATE

Work with your partner to plan how you will present your American Hero Poster to the class. Use the Presenting Checklist to help you make a strong presentation. Discuss the sentence starters below and write your answers.

An interesting fact I learned about this American hero is

_____

_____

I would like to know more about _____

_____

_____

WRITING

Expert Model

Features of a Biography

A biography teaches us about an important person and the events in his or her life.

- It tells about events in a person's life in sequence.

- It includes a conclusion.

Analyze an Expert Model Studying *Brave Bessie* will help you learn about writing a biography. Reread pages 395 in the **Literature Anthology**. Then answer the questions below.

What sensory words help you understand why Bessie was a little scared on her trip?

_____

_____

In the second paragraph, what words help show what it meant for Bessie to reach France?

_____

_____

Literature Anthology pages 390–401

Quick Tip

Remember that sensory words can tell about how something looks, feels, or sounds. Authors use sensory words to help readers visualize, or picture, an event.

Word Wise

The author uses the pronouns *she* and *her* in many details that tell about Bessie. Using both pronouns and nouns will make your writing easier to read.

Plan: Brainstorm

Generate Ideas You will write a biography about a hero. Draw and brainstorm ideas about people you think are heroes. Think about what you already know and what you want to learn about them. Use this space for your ideas.

Plan: Choose Your Topic

Writing Prompt Write a biography about someone you think is a hero. Remember, a hero is someone that people admire, or look up to. Use your ideas from page 25. Complete these sentences to help you get started.

The name of my hero is _____

This person is a hero because _____

_____

The biography will answer these questions about my hero:

_____

_____

_____

Purpose and Audience Authors write biographies to teach us about important people and events. Think about why you admire the person you want to write about. In your writer's notebook, explain why you want others to learn about your hero.

Plan: Organization

Primary and Secondary Sources You will research information about your hero. Using at least one primary source, such as something your hero wrote or said, can make your biography more interesting.

A writer listed primary and secondary sources to research information for a biography. Add an example of a primary source and secondary source to the chart.

Primary Sources	Secondary Sources
speech	encyclopedia
photograph	textbook

Plan Find at least one primary source and one secondary source for your biography. List your sources in your writer's notebook. Then take notes from your sources. Look for answers to the questions you wrote on page 26. You will use your notes to develop your ideas with specific details.

Draft

Sequence Authors often tell the events in a person's life in sequence, or in the order they happened. This helps readers to follow the events and understand why they happened. "César Chávez" is written in sequence. **Circle** words that show the order of two events in Cesar's life.

> When César was ten, it did not rain for a long time. This drought caused the plants on the farm to die. Without crops to sell, César's family couldn't afford to keep the farm.
>
> Then César's family moved to California where there was no drought.

Use the text above as a model to write about events in your hero's life in sequence.

_____

_____

_____

Quick Tip

Put events in the order that they happened. Words such as *first, next, then, later,* and *when* will help show the sequence.

You can use a timeline to show when events in your hero's life happened.

Grammar Connections

You may include the day of an event in the text. Write a comma between the day and the year in a date.

He won a gold medal on February 4, 1980.

Write a Draft Look over the notes you took from your sources. Organize the information in sequence to help you write a draft in your writer's notebook.

Revise

Strong Conclusions Authors may end a biography in an interesting way to help you remember what you have learned and understand why someone is important.

Reread the last paragraph on page 399 of *Brave Bessie* in the **Literature Anthology**. Talk about how the author ends the biography. How does this conclusion help you understand why Bessie Coleman is a hero?

_____

_____

_____

_____

_____

_____

 Revise It's time to revise your draft. Check that you wrote events in sequence. Make sure your conclusion helps readers understand why you admire your hero.

Grammar Connections

A subject pronoun tells who or what did an action.

She *traveled to France.*

They *learned to fly.*

An object pronoun comes after an action verb or a preposition.

Bessie's mom gave *her* *books to read.*

The wagon library rented books to *them*.

Revise: Peer Conferences

Review a Draft Listen carefully as a partner reads his or her work aloud. Begin by telling what you liked about the draft. Make suggestions that you think might make the writing stronger.

Partner Feedback Write one of your partner's suggestions that you will use in the revision of your biography.

Based on my partner's feedback, I will _____

_____

_____

After you finish giving each other feedback, reflect on the peer conference. What was helpful? What might you do differently next time?

_____

_____

 Revision Use the Revising Checklist to help you figure out what text you may need to move, add to, or delete. Remember to use the rubric on page 33 to help you with your revision.

✓ Revising Checklist

- ☐ Does the biography show why the person is a hero to others?
- ☐ Are the events in sequence?
- ☐ Did I use primary and secondary sources?
- ☐ Did I use pronouns such as *he, she, him,* and *her*?

Edit and Proofread

When you edit and proofread, you look for and correct mistakes in your writing. Rereading a revised draft several times will help you catch any errors. Use the checklist below to edit your sentences.

 Tech Tip

If you wrote on a computer, use the spell-check feature to help you find and correct spelling mistakes.

✔ Editing Checklist

☐ Do all sentences end with a punctuation mark?

☐ Do the subjects and verbs agree in all the sentences?

☐ Are all sentences complete sentences?

☐ Are subject, object, and possessive pronouns used correctly?

☐ Are commas used correctly in dates?

☐ Are all the words spelled correctly?

Grammar Connections

A possessive pronoun shows who or what owns something. Some possessive pronouns come before nouns.

*Bessie got **her** pilot's license.*

*Bessie flew the plane after she checked **its** wings and propeller.*

List two mistakes you found as you proofread your biography.

1 _____

_____

2 _____

_____

Publish, Present, and Evaluate

Publishing Create a clean, neat final copy of your biography. You may add a timeline, illustrations, or other visuals. Write a list of your primary and secondary sources at the end of your work.

Presentation Practice your presentation when you are ready to present your work. Use the Presenting Checklist to help you.

Evaluate After you publish and present your biography, use the rubric on the next page to evaluate your writing.

1 What did you do successfully? _____

_____

_____

2 What needs more work? _____

_____

_____

✓ Presenting Checklist

- ☐ Sit up or stand up straight.
- ☐ Look at the audience.
- ☐ Share information clearly.
- ☐ Speak at an appropriate pace—not too quickly or slowly.
- ☐ Carefully listen to your classmates' questions and respond with details from your biography.

Listening When you listen actively, you pay close attention to what you hear. When you listen to other presentations, take notes to help you better understand the ideas.

What I learned from ....'s
presentation:

_____

Questions I have about ....'s
presentation:

_____

✓ Listening Checklist

☐ Make eye contact with the speaker.

☐ Listen for details that answer questions about the topic.

☐ Identify what the speaker does well.

☐ Think of questions you can ask.

4	3	2	1
• tells a real person's life story and clearly explains why he or she is a hero • uses correct pronouns • uses primary and secondary sources • follows a sequence of events • is free or almost free from errors	• tells a real person's life story and gives some explanation why he or she is a hero • uses mostly correct pronouns • uses a primary and a secondary source • most events are in correct sequence • has few errors	• tells a real person's life story • uses some correct pronouns • uses at least one source • some events follow correct sequence • has frequent errors	• does not focus on the person • does not attempt to use pronouns • does not use sources • most events are not in sequence • many errors make the story difficult to understand

Playground Fundraiser

COLLABORATE

These girls are raising money to buy playground equipment. They are good citizens.

- A citizen shows responsibility by keeping the neighborhood clean.

- A citizen has rights, such as the right to go to school.

How can you be a good citizen? Talk with a partner. Write your ideas in the web.

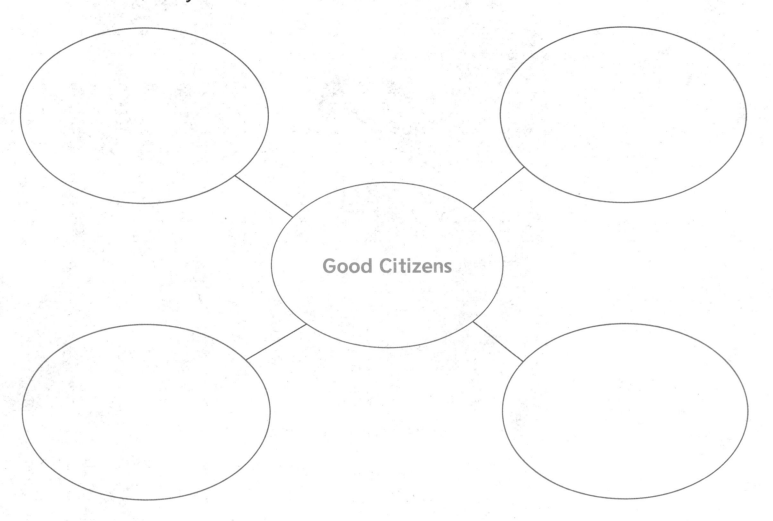

Good Citizens

Ryan Smith/Somos Images/Corbis

TAKE NOTES

Asking questions helps you figure out what you want to learn, or your purpose for reading. Write your questions here.

_____

_____

_____

_____

As you read, make note of:

Interesting Words _____

_____

_____

Key Details _____

_____

_____

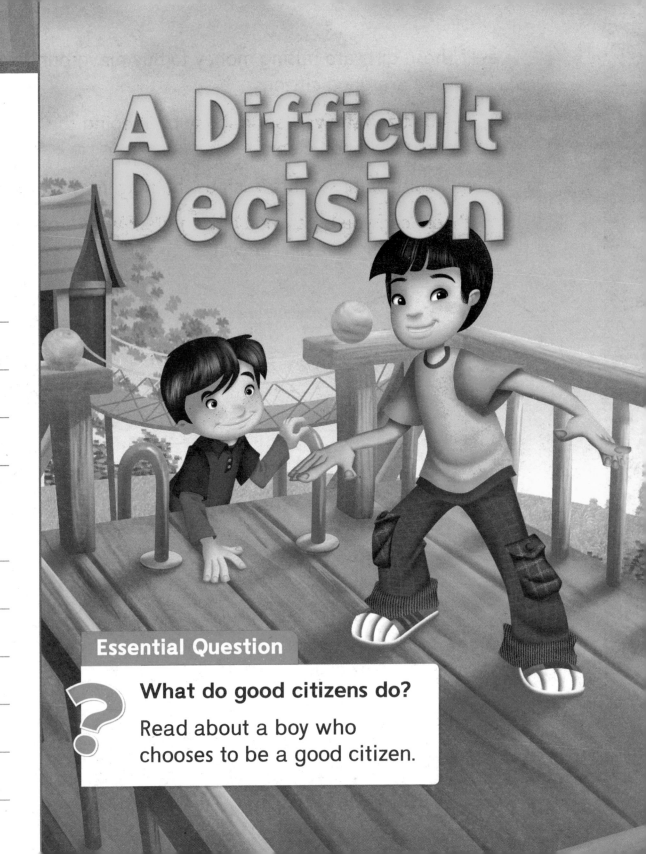

A Difficult Decision

Essential Question

? **What do good citizens do?**

Read about a boy who chooses to be a good citizen.

My best friend Paul and I were excited to go to the park after school. The park had a new fort. The Parks Department let the kids choose what kind of equipment to build, and the fort got the most **votes.** After school, Mom and I met Paul and his dad at the park.

Paul and I raced to the top of the tower. "I win. I'm the **champion,**" I shouted. "Look, Paul! Someone left the newest GameMaster here. It's mine now!"

Paul raised his eyebrows and looked thoughtful. "Wyatt, you cannot keep that GameMaster," he said. "You have a **responsibility** to return it. It is your duty!"

I asked, "Haven't you ever heard the saying, 'finders keepers, losers weepers'? I have **rights.** I found it, so I am claiming it."

Daniel Griffo

FIND TEXT EVIDENCE

Read

Paragraphs 1 and 2
First Person

Circle the pronouns that help show that the story is told in the first person.

Paragraph 3
Point of View
Underline the sentences that explain Paul's point of view about the GameMaster. What does Paul think Wyatt should do?

_____

_____

Reread

Author's Craft

How does the author use dialogue to show that the characters feel differently?

FIND TEXT EVIDENCE 🔍

Read

Paragraph 3

Make and Confirm Predictions

Underline the sentence that helps you make a prediction about what Wyatt will do with the GameMaster. Why does he decide to do this?

_____

_____

Paragraph 4

Point of View

Draw a box around the word that shows Paul thinks Wyatt made a good decision.

Reread

Author's Craft

How does the author use Paul's dialogue to help you understand Wyatt's traits?

"You can do whatever you want, Wyatt, but you know it's wrong to keep it," Paul said. Then he added, "Whenever there are **issues** like this at school, you're the one who helps solve the problems. Now you aren't taking your own advice."

Then Paul added, "I **volunteered** my thoughts. If you don't want to take the help I offered, there's nothing I can do."

Paul was right. I couldn't keep the game because it wasn't mine. The person who lost it would be upset. I cleared my throat and said in my best deep voice, "I've **determined** that you're right!"

"I'm delighted you decided to do the right thing," said Paul.

We told my mother what happened. She walked around the park with us so we could try to find the owner of the game. Soon we saw a boy and his Mom looking for something. He looked hopeless, and he burst into tears when we asked him if the game was his. "Yes," he wailed, "I lost my GameMaster a little while ago. I should have been more careful!"

Afterward, Mom and I walked home. I was glad I returned the toy to the boy. So, I made a **promise** to myself to always try to do the right thing. Now that is a vow I can keep!

Summarize

Use the most important details from "A Difficult Decision" to orally summarize what happens in the story.

FIND TEXT EVIDENCE

Read

Paragraph 1
Suffixes

Underline the word that means "without hope." **Circle** the word ending.

Paragraph 2
Make and Confirm Predictions

Confirm your prediction on page 38. How was it right?

_____

_____

_____

_____

Reread

Author's Craft

Why does the author include a description of the boy who lost the GameMaster?

Vocabulary

**Talk with a partner about each word.
Then answer the questions.**

champion

Maya won the game and became the
new **champion**.

What would you get if you were the champion of
a game?

_____

_____

determined

The boy **determined** which books to check
out at the library.

Who determined what you will read today?

_____

_____

> **Build Your Word List** Pick a word
> from the story. Use a thesaurus to look
> up synonyms and antonyms of the word.

issues

The teachers met to talk about important
school **issues**.

What are some important issues in your school?

_____

_____

promises

Zack and Jon made a **promise** to tell the
truth.

Why should you keep your promise?

_____

_____

responsibility

It is my **responsibility** to clean my room.

What is a responsibility you have at home?

_____

_____

rights

Going to school is one of your **rights** as a citizen.

What rights do you have?

_____

_____

volunteered

I **volunteered** to pick up trash in our park.

When is a time you volunteered to help?

_____

_____

votes

The teacher counted the **votes** for the class president.

Why do we use votes to decide things?

_____

_____

Suffixes

To figure out the meaning of a word you do not know, separate the root word from its suffix, such as: _care • less, help • ful, sharp • er, clean • est, select • ion._

🔍 **FIND TEXT EVIDENCE**

I'm not sure what thoughtful _means. The root word is_ thought, _which has to do with thinking about something. The suffix –ful means "full of." I think the word_ thoughtful _means "having a lot of thoughts."_

Paul raised his eyebrows and looked thoughtful.

Your Turn Use suffixes to figure out the meanings of the words from page 39 in "A Difficult Decision."

owner _____

careful _____

Make and Confirm Predictions

Use what you know about realistic fiction to help you predict, or guess, what might happen next. As you read, check to see if your predictions are correct.

🔍 FIND TEXT EVIDENCE

As you read page 38, use the realistic dialogue between the two boys to make a prediction about what Paul will say next.

Page 38

> Then Paul added, "I **volunteered** my thoughts. If you don't want to take the help I offered, there's nothing I can do."

I predict that Paul will say the right thing to convince Wyatt to return the GameMaster.

Your Turn When Wyatt saw the sad boy, what did you predict would happen? Confirm if your prediction is correct.

_____

_____

_____

As you read realistic fiction, think about how the characters do things like real people. Use details about how Wyatt and Paul act like real people to predict what will happen next. Confirm or correct any predictions you make.

First Person

"A Difficult Decision" is realistic fiction. Realistic fiction has characters, a setting, and events that could really happen. It can be told in the first person.

🔍 FIND TEXT EVIDENCE

I can tell that "A Difficult Decision" is realistic fiction. Wyatt and Paul act like real people. I also see that the story is told by Wyatt, in the first person.

Page 37

My best friend Paul and I were excited to go to the park after school. The park had a new fort. The Parks Department let the kids choose what kind of equipment to build, and the fort got the most **votes.** After school, Mom and I met Paul and his dad at the park.

Paul and I raced to the top of the tower. "I win. I'm the **champion,**" I shouted. "Look, Paul! Someone left the newest GameMaster here. It's mine now!"

Paul raised his eyebrows and looked thoughtful. "Wyatt, you cannot keep that GameMaster," he said. "You have a **responsibility** to return it. It is your duty!"

I asked, "Haven't you ever heard the saying, 'finders keepers, losers weepers'? I have **rights.** I found it, so I am claiming it."

Readers to Writers

When you write a story in the first person, ask yourself: *How does the first person help me show the character's thoughts and feelings?*

First Person

The story uses **first person** point of view. The character uses *I* and *my* to tell his thoughts and feelings.

COLLABORATE

Your Turn Why did the author write in the first person? How does this help you understand the main character?

_____

_____

_____

_____

Point of View

A character telling the story has feelings about the events. This is the character's point of view. The words *I, my, me,* and *mine* tell who is speaking.

🔍 FIND TEXT EVIDENCE

When I read the second paragraph on page 37 of "A Difficult Decision," I can tell Wyatt is talking. I will look for clues to his point of view.

Character	Clue	Point of View
Wyatt	"It's mine, now!"	In the beginning of the story, Wyatt thinks he should keep a game he found.

Your Turn Continue rereading the story. Fill in the graphic organizer to show how Wyatt's point of view changes from the beginning to the middle to the end of the story.

Daniel Griffo

Character	Clue	Point of View
Wyatt	"It's mine, now!"	In the beginning of the story, Wyatt thinks he should keep a game he found.

Respond to Reading

COLLABORATE

Talk about the prompt below. Think about how the author shows Wyatt's thoughts and feelings. Use your notes and graphic organizer.

What does Wyatt learn about being a good citizen?
Why is this lesson important for all citizens?

_____

_____

_____

_____

_____

_____

_____

_____

RESEARCH AND INQUIRY

Ask and Answer Questions

When you research a topic, begin by asking questions. You will use what you already know and learn new facts to answer your questions. Focus your research on finding those answers.

Research and compare the roles of a city mayor, a state governor, and the U.S. President. Remember to begin by asking questions. What questions do you have about these leaders?

The governor of Texas works in this building.

_____

_____

_____

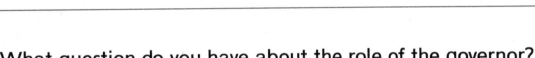

What question do you have about the role of the governor?

_____

COLLABORATE

Create a Pamphlet Choose one of these roles. Work with a partner to create a pamphlet. Describe why you would be a good mayor, governor, or president. Tell what you would do for the people.

Role: _____

Quick Tip

As you ask and answer questions, think about what you already know, what you want to know, and what you learned and how all this information helps you with the questions.

Grace for President

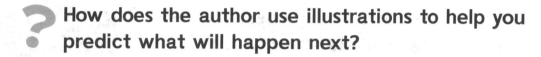

How does the author use illustrations to help you predict what will happen next?

Literature Anthology: pages 406–427

COLLABORATE

Talk About It Reread page 408. Talk about what Grace says and what is on the wall behind her.

Quick Tip

As you read, look for clues in both the text and the illustrations to help you make predictions.

Cite Text Evidence Write clues from the text and the illustration. Then write how they show what will happen next.

> Clue from Text

> What happens next?

> Clue from Illustration

Make Inferences

How is Grace feeling? How do the text and illustrations help you infer how Grace feels?

Write The author uses illustrations to help you predict

_____

_____

? **What does the author's placement of the illustrations show you about the campaigns?**

 Talk About It Reread pages 413–414. Talk about how the illustrations are placed and what they show.

Cite Text Evidence Write details about Grace's campaign, Thomas's campaign, and both campaigns.

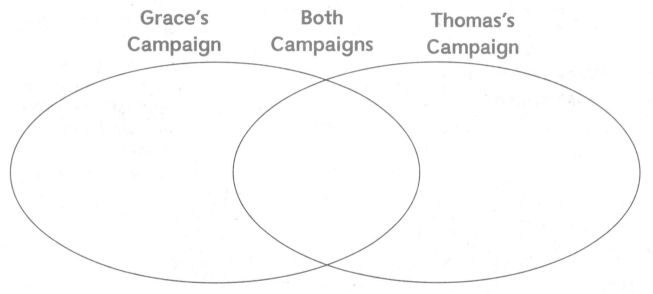

Grace's Campaign | Both Campaigns | Thomas's Campaign

Write The author places the illustrations to show

_____

_____

_____

? **Why does the author end the page with only one state's votes unaccounted for?**

Talk About It Reread pages 421–422. Talk about how the author ends page 422.

Cite Text Evidence In the circles below, write three reasons the author ends the page with Wyoming.

Reread pages 421–422.

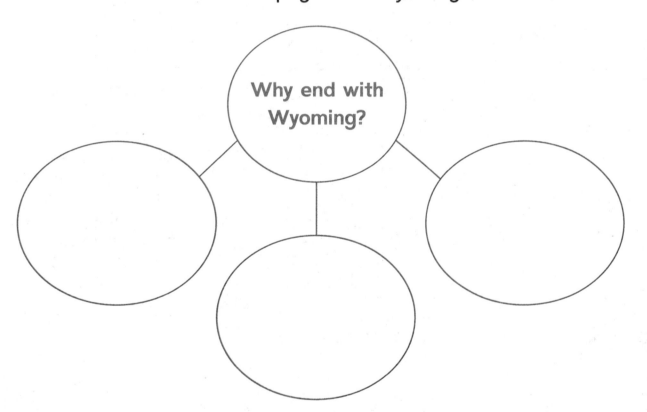

Why end with Wyoming?

Write The author ends the page this way to _____

_____

DSGpro/Getty Images

Respond to Reading

COLLABORATE

Discuss the prompt below. Summarize what has happened in the story so far to help you answer the question.

How does the author keep the reader interested in the story about Grace's run for class president?

_____

_____

_____

_____

_____

_____

_____

_____

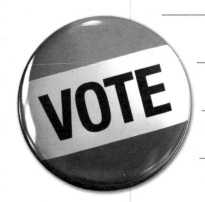

Quick Tip

Use these sentence starters to tell how the author keeps the reader interested in the story.

The author uses text and illustrations to...

The author helps the reader predict what happens next by...

The author builds interest by...

Self-Selected Reading

Choose a text. In your writer's notebook, write the title, author, and genre of the book. As you read, make a connection to ideas in other texts you read or to a personal experience. Write your ideas in your writer's notebook.

Helping to Make Smiles

*Literature Anthology:
pages 428–429*

Camp Smiles

During the summer, Matthew goes to Camp Smiles. It is an Easter Seals camp for children with disabilities. Children with special needs often can't go to other camps. Other camps cannot help them meet their needs. At Camp Smiles there is special gear. Each camper has a buddy to help him or her. Children at Camp Smiles are able to ride horses, play basketball, and swim. Camp may be the only place where they can do those activities.

Reread the paragraph. **Underline** the sentence with information the author gives about Camp Smiles and the campers who go there.

Circle what campers can do at Camp Smiles.

Discuss why Camp Smiles is a special place. Write evidence from the paragraph that supports your answer.

_____

_____

_____

_____

Matthew's Camp Challenge

Matthew had a great time at Camp Smiles. He wanted other kids like him to go to camp. Not all kids can afford to go to camp. Matthew wanted to change that. He decided to challenge people to give money. The money will pay for 30 children to go to Camp Smiles. Matthew showed responsibility. He is involved in his community. He is helping to make children with disabilities smile.

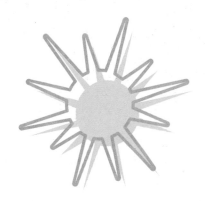

Reread the paragraph. **Underline** two ways Matthew is a good citizen. Explain them here.

_____

_____

Circle how Matthew helped pay for more kids to go to camp.

COLLABORATE

With a partner, discuss what *community* means in this selection. What communities is Matthew involved with? Write your answer here.

_____

_____

_____

_____

? **Why did the author choose "Helping to Make Smiles" as a title for this selection?**

Quick Tip

As you reread to answer questions, look for examples in the text to support your answers.

Talk About It Talk about the different ways people in the community help children with disabilities.

Cite Text Evidence Write about the different people who bring smiles to the campers and how those people help.

People	How They Help

Write The author chose the title name because

_____

_____

_____

_____

Graphic Features and Callouts

A callout is a short piece of text that has larger type or different type. Authors use graphic features such as callouts to give more information about a topic.

FIND TEXT EVIDENCE

Reread the callout on page 429. Think about why the author uses a callout for this information. Answer the questions below.

What is the title of the callout? _____

What makes someone a good citizen?

- _____   - _____

- _____   - _____

Your Turn Why do you think the author put this information in a callout?

_____

_____

_____

Quick Tip

As you read nonfiction such as "Helping to Make Smiles," look for information in the text and graphic features. Authors can use callouts to share information not found in the main part of the text. Think about what this information adds to the topic.

? What have you learned from the selections you read and the song "America the Beautiful" about being a good citizen?

Talk About It Discuss what it means for a citizen to sing the song "America the Beautiful."

COLLABORATE

Cite Text Evidence **Circle** details in the song that help you understand what is beautiful about America. Talk about what good citizens do to keep America beautiful.

Write Stories and songs like "America the Beautiful" show us

_____

_____

_____

Quick Tip

When you read, it helps to think about how you can make connections between texts. You can ask yourself: how are the ideas in the texts similar and different?

America the Beautiful

O beautiful for spacious skies,
For amber waves of grain.
For purple mountain majesties,
Above the fruited plain.
America! America!

God shed His grace on thee,
And crown thy good with brotherhood,
From sea to shining sea.

— Music by Samuel Ward
— Words by Katharine Lee Bates

pbokerp/iStock/Getty Images

Present Your Work

With your partner or group, plan how you will present your pamphlet to the class. Discuss the sentence starters below and write your answers.

A _____ does many things, including

_____

I would like to learn more about how leaders _____

_____

_____

Talk About It

COLLABORATE

These children are going on a class trip. They are following the school rules. They walk in line and listen to their teacher.

Rules and laws keep people, animals, and property safe. Talk to a partner about rules that you have at school or at home. Share your information using complete sentences. Why are these rules important? Write your ideas in the chart.

Rule	Why It Is Important

Edward Parker/Alamy Stock Photo

TAKE NOTES

Asking questions helps you figure out what you want to learn. Questions help you gain information. Write your questions here.

_____

_____

_____

As you read, make note of:

Interesting Words _____

_____

_____

Key Details _____

_____

_____

The Problem with PLASTIC BAGS

Essential Question

? Why are rules important?

Read about whether there should be rules for recycling plastic bags.

Blend Images/Getty Images

or most Americans, plastic bags are part of shopping. Often these bags get thrown away soon after the trip to the store. About 500 billion bags are produced each year around the world. Fewer than 3% are recycled. This has a serious impact on the environment.

Some U.S. cities have created **rules** that ban plastic bags in stores. But not everyone is **united** behind these laws. People argue that we can continue to use plastic bags and still have the ability to protect the planet.

FIND TEXT EVIDENCE

Read

Paragraph 1
Multiple Meaning Words
Circle the words that help you understand what "trip" means.

Paragraph 2
Summarize
Underline how some cities are dealing with plastic bags. Summarize how people feel about this issue.

_____

_____

_____

Reread

Author's Craft

Why does the author include facts with numbers about plastic bags?

TIME FOR KIDS

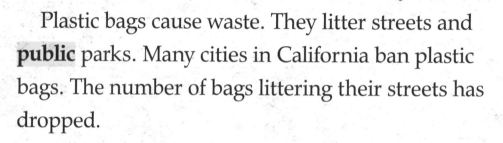

FIND TEXT EVIDENCE

Read

Paragraph 1

Evaluate Information

Why did the number of bags littering the streets of California drop? **Draw a box** around the sentence that helps you explain this.

Fluency

Reread "The Problem with Plastic Bags." Change the tone of your voice to express the opinions, thoughts, and feelings of the author.

Reread

Author's Craft

How does the author use facts and opinions to persuade the reader?

We Should Ban Plastic Bags

Plastic bags cause waste. They litter streets and **public** parks. Many cities in California ban plastic bags. The number of bags littering their streets has dropped.

Plastic bags pollute our land and water. This hurts wildlife. Some fish and birds can mistake the plastic for food. This may cause serious health problems and other dangers for the animals.

It takes resources to make plastic bags. We need to **finally** limit our use of plastic to save these resources. A ban will help shoppers **form** the habit of bringing reusable bags to stores.

We Still Need Plastic Bags

Let's look at **history** and learn from our mistakes. We don't need a ban. We need better ways to recycle. Many stores are now helping to make recycling easier. They put out bins for plastic bags. This limits litter and pollution. It also helps save Earth's resources.

Writers of laws to ban plastic bags do not understand how it hurts shoppers. Plastic bags are convenient. People cannot carry reusable bags at all times. It costs money to buy reusable bags. People have **exclaimed** they need those dollars to spend on their families.

Reasons to Ban Plastic Bags	Reasons to Keep Plastic Bags
Less waste and litter	Convenient to use
Protects animals	Can be recycled
Saves Earth's resources	Saves customers money

Summarize

Use the most important facts to orally summarize each side of the argument about banning plastic bags.

(t)McGraw-Hill Education,(b)LordRunar/iStock/Getty Images

PERSUASIVE ARTICLE

FIND TEXT EVIDENCE

Read

Paragraph 2

Author's Purpose

Circle the two reasons the author gives that support not banning plastic bags. Write the two reasons here.

_____

_____

_____

Charts

Look at the chart. **Underline** a fact in each column that gives information about helping the planet.

Reread

Author's Craft

Why does the author use a chart to summarize two sides of the argument?

Vocabulary

**Talk with a partner about each word.
Then answer the questions.**

exclaimed

"What a fun surprise!" James **exclaimed**.

How do you think James felt when he exclaimed about the surprise?

_____

_____

finally

Jen **finally** learned how to dive.

What is something that you finally learned how to do?

_____

_____

> **Build Your Word List** Reread paragraph 1 on page 61. Circle *shopping*. Use a word web to write other forms for this word.

form

Charlie and Amy want to **form** a chess club.

What kind of club would you like to form?

_____

_____

history

Ben learned about the **history** of his family.

What is something in history you want to learn about?

_____

_____

public

The park is Gina's favorite **public** place.

What public place do you like to visit?

_____

_____

rules

We must follow the rules in the gym.

What is a a rule at your school?

_____

_____

united

The team united to win the game.

Why is it important for a team to be united?

_____

_____

writers

The writers finished their stories.

Name a famous writer who lived long ago.

_____

_____

Multiple Meaning Words

As you read, you may find words that could have more than one meaning. The other words in the sentence will help you figure out which meaning is correct.

FIND TEXT EVIDENCE

On page 62 of "The Problem with Plastic Bags," I see the word save. _I know that_ save _means "to help someone from danger." It can also mean "to keep something." When I read the sentence, the meaning "to keep something" makes sense._

We need to finally limit our use of plastic to save these resources.

Your Turn Write the correct meaning of each word from page 62 below, based on the sentence.

parks _____

land _____

McGraw-Hill Education

Summarize

When you summarize, you use your own words to retell the most important information in a text. Summarizing helps you understand what you read.

🔍 FIND TEXT EVIDENCE

After reading the first paragraph of "The Problem with Plastic Bags," I can summarize the important points.

Page 61

For most Americans, plastic bags are part of shopping. Often these bags get thrown away soon after the trip to the store. About 500 billion bags are produced each year around the world. Fewer than 3% are recycled. This has a serious impact on the environment.

People use billions of plastic bags every year. Few are recycled. This hurts the environment.

Your Turn Write a summary of paragraph 1 on page 63.

_____

_____

_____

Charts

"The Problem with Plastic Bags" is a persuasive article. It states an opinion about a topic. It has facts and examples to support the opinion. Persuasive texts often include text features, such as charts.

🔍 FIND TEXT EVIDENCE

I can tell that "The Problem with Plastic Bags" is a persuasive article because it gives facts and opinions. It uses facts and examples to convince someone to feel a certain way about a ban on plastic bags. The text also has a chart.

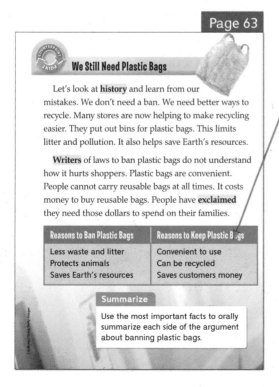

Page 63

We Still Need Plastic Bags

Let's look at **history** and learn from our mistakes. We don't need a ban. We need better ways to recycle. Many stores are now helping to make recycling easier. They put out bins for plastic bags. This limits litter and pollution. It also helps save Earth's resources.

Writers of laws to ban plastic bags do not understand how it hurts shoppers. Plastic bags are convenient. People cannot carry reusable bags at all times. It costs money to buy reusable bags. People have **exclaimed** they need those dollars to spend on their families.

Reasons to Ban Plastic Bags	Reasons to Keep Plastic Bags
Less waste and litter	Convenient to use
Protects animals	Can be recycled
Saves Earth's resources	Saves customers money

Summarize

Use the most important facts to orally summarize each side of the argument about banning plastic bags.

Chart

A chart is a list of information that is shown in rows. The heading tells that these facts explain why plastic bags should not be banned.

Your Turn Why does the author include a chart in the article?

_____

_____

_____

Author's Purpose

Authors can write a text for many different reasons. A text can explain, describe, or try to persuade the reader to think a certain way.

🔍 FIND TEXT EVIDENCE

As I reread page 62 of "The Problem with Plastic Bags," I identify the facts and examples. I see that cities that ban plastic bags have less litter now. I can use this fact as a clue to figure out the author's purpose for writing "We Should Ban Plastic Bags."

Clue
Litter has dropped in cities that ban plastic bags.

 Your Turn Reread page 62. Fill in the graphic organizer to help you identify the author's purpose using clues found in the selection.

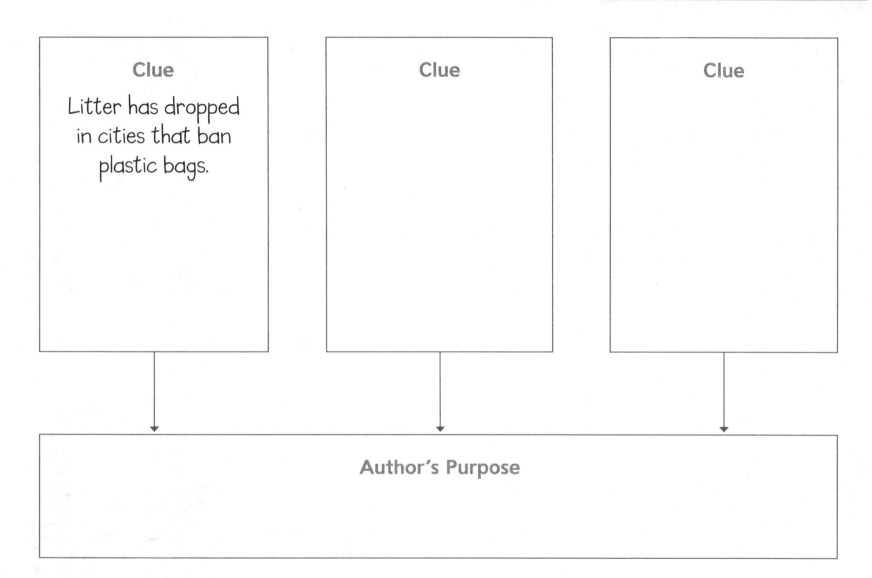

Clue	Clue	Clue
Litter has dropped in cities that ban plastic bags.		

Author's Purpose

Respond to Reading

COLLABORATE

Talk about the prompt below. Think about the text features the author uses. Use your notes and graphic organizer.

How does the author persuade you to agree or disagree with a ban on plastic bags?

_____

_____

_____

_____

_____

_____

_____

Quick Tip

Use these sentence starters to help you organize your text evidence.

Plastic bags are/ are not a problem because...

I think we should...

The reasons I think this are...

McGraw-Hill Education

Find and Gather Sources

To research a topic, you need to find sources that have information about your topic. You can use print sources, such as books and magazines, or Internet websites.

To find sources, you can do an online search. Type in words about your topic. For example, if you want to find sources about recycling plastic bags, type in *recycling plastic* or *recycle.*

What words would you type in to search for sources about composting?

_____

Recycling Chart With a partner, create a recycling chart with the heads "Paper, Plastic, and Metal." Use sources to find information about what types of objects can be recycled in each section. Make a drawing of an object from the chart that can be recycled.

What questions could you ask to learn about what can be recycled?

_____

_____

Paper	Plastic	Metal

A Call to Compost

 ? **How does the author use headings to organize "A Call to Compost?"**

Literature Anthology: pages 430–433

Talk About It Look back at pages 430–433. Talk about the way the author organizes the information in the article.

Cite Text Evidence In the boxes below, list the heads that the author uses to organize the article. Then tell what each section is about.

 Make Inferences

Why do you think the author included the chart on page 433? How does this chart help the reader?

Heads	What this Section is About
Chart Head	**What this Chart is About**

Write The author uses headings because _____

_____

_____

? **Why does the author give details to support each argument about composting?**

COLLABORATE

Talk About It Reread p. 431-432. Talk about the reasons the author gives to support each argument.

Cite Text Evidence In the boxes below, list three reasons the author gives to support each argument.

Composting Should Be a Law	Composting Should Be a Choice

Write The author gives details for both arguments because

_____

_____

GaryAlvis/E+/Getty Images

Respond to Reading

Discuss the prompt below. Talk about the two arguments the author shares about composting. Then answer the questions.

Do you think composting should be a law or a choice? What details did the author give to persuade you?

_____

_____

_____

_____

_____

_____

_____

Quick Tip

Use these sentence frames to organize your text evidence.

One detail the author gave about composting is...

Another detail the author gave is...

These details convinced me because...

Self-Selected Reading

Choose a text. In your writer's notebook, write the title, author, and genre of the book. As you read, make a connection to ideas in other texts you read, or a personal experience. Write your ideas in your writer's notebook.

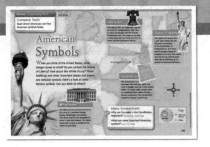

American Symbols

Literature Anthology:
pages 434–435

The Liberty Bell was originally ordered as a bell for Independence Hall. That is where the people who formed the Constitution met. The crack in the bell is more than two feet long! Just like its name, the bell symbolizes liberty.

The Statue of Liberty was a gift from France for the 100-year anniversary of the Declaration of Independence. It is a symbol of freedom and hope.

Reread the paragraphs. **Circle** the two American symbols the author describes.

Which symbol was a gift from France? Why was it a gift?

_____

_____

COLLABORATE

Talk with a partner about why these two symbols are important to Americans. Write evidence from the text that supports your answer.

_____

_____

_____

(t)Tetra Images/Getty Images;(b)Image Source/Getty Images

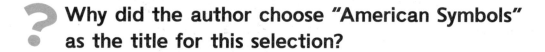

? **Why did the author choose "American Symbols" as the title for this selection?**

Talk About It Talk about what the two symbols have in common.

Cite Text Evidence Reread the selection. Write what the author says that the items symbolize.

Quick Tip

As you read, look at the headings to help you find the information you need.

Symbol	This symbolizes...
Liberty Bell	
Statue of Liberty	

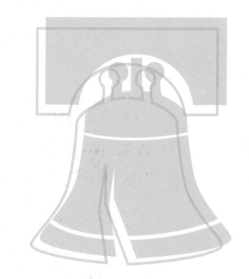

Write The author chose "American Symbols" as the title

because _____

_____

_____

Print and Graphic Features

Authors write informational text to share information. Sometimes authors include graphic features, such as photos and illustrations, to help their readers understand the text.

Reread "American Symbols." Look at the illustrations. Answer the questions below.

What illustrations does the author provide?

_____

_____

How do the illustrations help you?

_____

_____

Your Turn Reread "A Call to Compost." What illustrations could the author add to give more information to the reader?

_____

_____

When writing an informational text, consider adding a photo or illustration to help your readers better understand your topic.

? **What have you learned from the selections you read and the poem about why rules are important?**

COLLABORATE

Talk About It Read the poem "At Table" below. Then talk about how manners are rules for our families.

Cite Text Evidence **Circle** the parts in the poem that tell something a person with good manners would not do.

Write The selections I read and the poem show me that

rules are important because _____

_____

_____

"At Table" from *More Goops and How Not to Be Them*

Why is it Goops must always wish
To touch *each* apple on the dish?
Why do they never neatly fold
Their napkins until they are told?

Why do they play with food, and bite
Such awful mouthfuls? Is it right?
Why do they tilt back in their chairs?
Because they're Goops! So no one cares!

— Gelett Burgess

Intonation

Reading with intonation is changing the tone of your voice. Saying some words in a different tone will help express the meaning of what you are reading. When you read slowly, you show what words are more important. When you read some words a little louder, you show excitement.

Page 62

Plastic bags pollute our land and water. This hurts wildlife. Some fish and birds can mistake the plastic for food. This may cause serious health problems for the animals.

Use your voice to make this sentence sound important.

Your Turn Turn back to page 63. Take turns reading each paragraph of "We Still Need Plastic Bags" with a partner. Use your voice to express which ideas are important. Afterward, think about how you did. Complete these sentences.

I remembered to _____

Next time I will _____

_____

Quick Tip

Read at a rate, or speed, that is easy for listeners to understand. Try not to read too slowly or quickly. To read with accuracy, practice saying words you find difficult to pronounce.

Literature Anthology:
pages 430–433

Expert Model

Features of a Persuasive Essay

Authors write persuasive essays to give an opinion about a topic. A **persuasive essay**:

- supports an opinion with facts and details.

- often tries to get the reader to think a certain way, or take action.

Analyze an Expert Model Studying *A Call to Compost* will help you learn how to write a persuasive essay. Reread pages 430–431 in the **Literature Anthology**.

The author says governments should have laws requiring people to recycle food waste. What facts and details support this opinion?

_____

_____

How does the author try to get the reader to change his or her mind or take action?

_____

_____

Word Wise

The author uses persuasive words such as *should* and *should not* when giving an opinion. The author also uses strong words and phrases such as *giant piles, pollute, force,* and *smelly* to persuade the reader.

Plan: Brainstorm

Generate Ideas You will write a persuasive essay. Describe something you would like to change at school, such as a school rule or event. Explain why you want to make this change and how the change would make your school better. Use this space for your ideas. Brainstorm words about the rules and events at your school. Later, you will choose one rule or event from your list to write about.

Tatiana Popova/Shutterstock.com

Plan: Choose Your Topic

Writing Prompt Write a persuasive essay that states your opinion about what you want to change at school. Include reasons why you want to make this change and how it would help. Go back to the list of school rules and events that you brainstormed. Choose one of these rules or events. Complete these sentences to help you get started.

I would like to change _____

_____

I think it should be changed because _____

_____

This change will be good for everyone because _____

_____

Purpose and Audience Often, authors write persuasive essays to change readers' minds about a topic. Think about why you chose the rule or event you want to write about. Then explain your purpose for writing in your writer's notebook.

Neustockimages/Getty Images

Plan: Voice

Persuasive Language Often, an author uses persuasive language and strong words when trying to state a clear opinion about something. Look at the chart below. Fill in the last row with additional examples of persuasive and strong words. Pay attention to how the words relate to the topic.

Topic: Art and music programs in schools

Persuasive Words	Strong Words
I believe	Creative
This is important	Inspiring
This should	Fun

 Plan In your writer's notebook, use literal language to make a chart like the one shown above. Write persuasive and strong words you can use for the school rule or event you want to change.

Draft

Ideas: Develop a Topic The author of the "Point" section in "The Problem with Plastic Bags" begins by stating an opinion. Then the writer gives facts and relevant details. These facts and details help support an idea related to the topic.

POINT: We Should Ban Plastic Bags
Plastic bags cause waste. They litter streets and public parks.

Reread this section on page 62. Use it as a model to develop the topic in your essay. Write the beginning of your essay below. Explain your opinion and include a fact or relevant detail to support it.

_____

_____

_____

Write a Draft Look at your words that show the use of persuasive language. Use these words as you write the draft in your notebook. Remember to tell what you would like to change, and explain why you want to change it.

ludovikus/Shutterstock.com

Revise

Voice The author's opinion is how he or she feels about a topic. Words like *must, have to,* or *should* make the author's voice sound strong. Read the paragraph below. Then revise it to make the author's opinion sound powerful and clear.

> Right now we can only check out one library book at a time.
>
> We want to take out more books. Let's do something to make
>
> a change.

Grammar Connections

As you revise, make sure you use personal pronouns to tell about yourself. The words *I* and *me* tell just about you. The words *we* and *us* tell about you and other people.

_____

_____

_____

_____

 Revise It's time to revise your draft. Make sure you have clearly stated your opinion. Check to see that you used persuasive language.

Revise: Peer Conferences

Review a Draft Listen carefully as a partner reads his or her work aloud. Begin by telling what you like about the draft. Make suggestions that you think will make the writing stronger.

Partner Feedback Write one of your partner's suggestions that you will use in the revision of your text.

Based on my partner's feedback, I will _____

_____

_____

After you finish giving each other feedback, reflect on the peer conference. What was helpful? What might you do differently next time?

_____

_____

 Revision Use the Revising Checklist to help you figure out what text you may need to move, add to, or delete. Remember to use the rubric on page 89 to help you with your revision.

Quick Tip

Use these sentence starters to discuss your partner's work.
Your opinion...
Your use of persuasive words...
Your voice is...

✓ Revising Checklist

- ☐ Does my persuasive essay state my opinion?
- ☐ Does it include facts and details?
- ☐ Does it try to convince others to agree with me?
- ☐ Is there persuasive language?
- ☐ Did I use strong words?

Edit and Proofread

When you **edit** and **proofread**, you look for and correct mistakes in your writing. Rereading a revised draft several times will help you catch any errors. Use the checklist below to edit your sentences.

 Editing Checklist

- ☐ Do all sentences begin with a capital letter and end with a punctuation mark?
- ☐ Are all the words spelled correctly?
- ☐ Are proper nouns capitalized?
- ☐ Are pronouns used correctly?
- ☐ Are contractions spelled and used correctly?

List two mistakes you found as you proofread your text.

1 _____

2 _____

Digital Tools

For more information on opinion writing, watch the "Purpose of Opinion Writing" slide show. Go to **my.mheducation.com.**

 Tech Tip

When you type your text, hold the "shift" key while you press another key to make a capital letter.

Grammar Connections

As you proofread, make sure each sentence starts with a capital letter and ends with a punctuation mark. Remember to capitalize proper nouns. A proper noun names a particular person, place, or thing.

Publish, Present, and Evaluate

Publishing Create a neat, clean final copy of your persuasive essay. As you write your draft, be sure to print neatly and legibly. Leave the space of a pencil point between letters and the space of a pencil between words. You may add illustrations or other visuals to make your published work more interesting.

Presentation Practice your presentation when you are ready to present your work. Use the Presenting Checklist to help you.

Evaluate After you publish and present your persuasive essay, use the rubric on the next page to evaluate your writing.

1 What did you do successfully? _____

_____

_____

2 What needs more work? _____

_____

_____

✔ **Presenting Checklist**

☐ Sit up or stand up straight.
☐ Look at different people in the audience.
☐ Speak in a polite but strong voice.
☐ Put emphasis on your opinion words, like *must* and *should*.
☐ Answer questions using facts from your persuasive essay.

Listening When you listen actively, you pay close attention to what you hear. When you listen to other students' presentations, take notes to help you better understand their ideas.

What I learned from ....'s presentation:

_____

Questions I have about ....'s presentation:

_____

4	3	2	1
• clearly and strongly states an opinion • uses many facts and details to develop the topic • includes many examples of persuasive language • uses personal pronouns correctly • is free or almost free of errors	• mentions an opinion, but not in clear or strong manner • uses some facts and details to develop the topic • includes some examples of persuasive language • most personal pronouns are used correctly • has few errors	• does not clearly state an opinion • uses few facts and details to develop the topic • includes only one or two examples of persuasive language • some personal pronouns are used correctly • has frequent errors	• does not state an opinion • does not use facts and details to develop the topic • does not include persuasive language • personal pronouns are missing or used incorrectly • many errors make the writing hard to understand

Spiral Review

You have learned new skills and strategies in Unit 5 that will help you to read and understand texts. Now it is time to practice what you have learned.

- **Synonyms**
- **Suffixes**
- **Multiple-Meaning Words**
- **Sequence**
- **Point of View**
- **Author's Purpose**
- **Timeline**

Connect to Content

- **Persuasive Letter**
- **Respond to the Read Aloud**
- **Create a Timeline**

Read the selection and choose the best answer to each question.

George Washington Carver

1. When are peanuts more than peanuts? It's when they become milk or even soap. Scientist and teacher George Washington Carver discovered hundreds of uses for peanuts.

2. Carver was born in the early 1860s. He grew up on a farm in Missouri. His mother was a slave. Carver left home as a boy to find work and go to school.

3. He had an interest in <u>farming</u>. He attended college. There, Carver studied the science of agriculture. He became head of the agriculture program at Tuskegee University in Alabama.

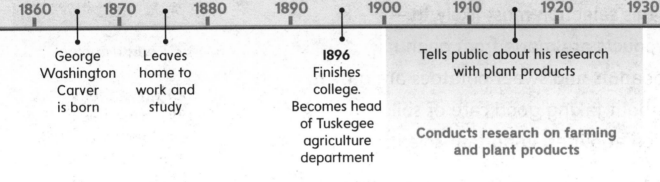

| 1860 | 1870 | 1880 | 1890 | 1900 | 1910 | 1920 | 1930 | 1940 | 1950 |

George Washington Carver is born

Leaves home to work and study

1896 Finishes college. Becomes head of Tuskegee agriculture department

Tells public about his research with plant products

Conducts research on farming and plant products

1943 Carver dies on January 5

4 Carver worked to help black farmers in the South. He taught them how to take better care of the soil. He urged them to plant peanuts and sweet potatoes instead of cotton.

5 Carver looked for new ways to use peanuts and sweet potatoes. He found that peanuts could be used to make flour. They could become inks and dyes. They could become face creams and medicines. By the 1940s, peanuts were a major crop in the country.

6 He also found that sweet potatoes could be used to make vinegar, glue, and other products. Farmers made money from these crops.

7 Carver improved farming and the lives of farmers. He won many awards for his work. Carver is seen as a hero to many people.

C Squared Studios/Getty Images

SHOW WHAT YOU LEARNED

1 The author wrote this selection most likely to —

  A explain how products are made from peanuts

  B describe how peanuts and sweet potatoes are grown

  C teach readers about taking good care of soil

  D share information about an important scientist

2 The author begins the selection with a question in order to —

  F find out how much readers already know

  G interest readers in the subject of the selection

  H entertain readers with a funny thought

  J remind readers to ask questions as they read the selection

3 What word in paragraph 3 means almost the same as <u>farming</u>?

  A interest

  B science

  C agriculture

  D program

4 According to the timeline, what important event happened in 1896?

  F George Washington Carver was born.

  G Carver left home to find work and to study.

  H Carver finished college and began his work.

  J Carver began sharing his research with the public.

Read the selection and choose the best answer to each question.

Dad for Mayor!

1   Dad likes helping our community. He served on the school <u>board</u>. Now, he wants to be mayor. That's like being the town president!

2   "I'll need a strong team," he told Mom. "I need help writing speeches. We need posters and people to call voters."

3   I knew that Dad wanted a team of grownups, but why couldn't kids be on his team? I didn't say anything yet. I had a plan.

4   At school, we were learning about elections. Our teacher said, "Voting is a way for your voice to be heard." She said voters should understand how governments work and what the key issues are. Some issues in our town are repairing the downtown bridge and making bike lanes. We also need a new library.

5   My friends and I met after school. We talked about improving our town. We sketched ideas for posters and listed reasons to vote for my dad. Then we listed reasons why voters should be a part of his team.

6   I showed Mom and Dad our ideas. "Even if we can't vote," I said, "we can still have a voice." They were amazed. Dad said, "How <u>thoughtless</u> of me not to include you to help with the election!"

7   Thirty people worked on Dad's team. We learned a lot about elections. Can you guess the best part? Dad won, thanks to his great team!

1 Read the dictionary entry.

Which meaning of <u>board</u> is used in paragraph 1?

A Meaning 1   **C** Meaning 3

B Meaning 2   **D** Meaning 4

2 Look at the diagram below.

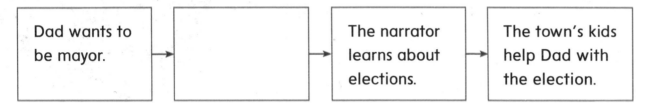

| Dad wants to be mayor. | | The narrator learns about elections. | The town's kids help Dad with the election. |

Which of the following completes the diagram?

F Dad wins the election.

G The narrator wants to be on Dad's team.

H Dad serves on the school board.

J The narrator meets with friends after school.

3 In paragraph 6, the word <u>thoughtless</u> means —

A not thinking carefully   **C** not thinking again

B thinking clearly   **D** thinking again

4 In the story, the author shows Dad's belief that —

F kids should not be part of his team

G he will probably win the election

H the town needs a new library

J he needs the help of a good team

board \bôrd\
noun

1. a long, flat piece of wood

2. what a surfer stands on

3. a group that makes decisions

4. a surface to play games on

Comparing Genres

Reread the biography "César Chávez" on pages 2–5.

- How does the author show that this is a true story about a real person?

_____

_____

_____

César Chávez

Review the realistic fiction story "A Difficult Decision" on pages 36–39.

- How are Wyatt and Paul like people you might know in real life?

_____

_____

_____

Talk about how the authors of both selections write about the real person and the characters. Then complete the Graphic Organizer on page 97 to show how the two genres are alike and different.

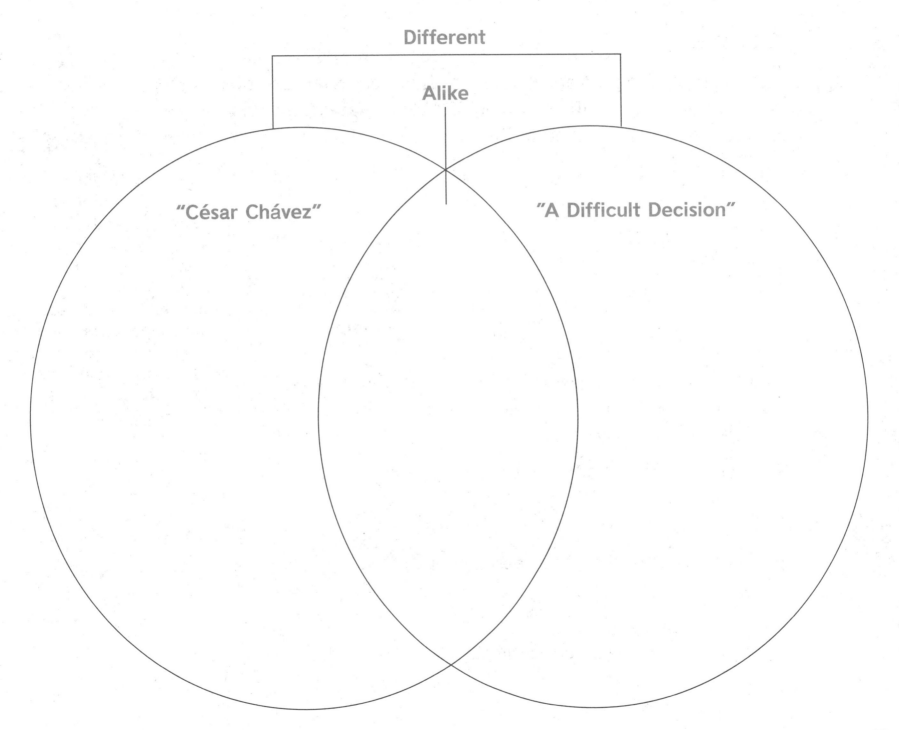

Different

Alike

"César Chávez"

"A Difficult Decision"

EXTEND YOUR LEARNING

Suffixes

A suffix is a word part or syllable that is added to the end of a word. To figure out the meaning of a word that has a suffix, add together the meaning of the root word and the suffix.

The chart below shows some suffixes and their meanings.

Suffix	Meaning
-ful	full of
-ly	in a certain way
-less	without

Read the sentences below. Circle the words that have suffixes. Use the information in the chart to help you write what each circled word means.

- I saw a picture of a hairless cat.

_____

- She quietly watched the sleeping puppy.

_____

- Be careful when you cross the street.

_____

Quick Tip

The word endings -s, -es, -ed, and -ing are not suffixes. These endings answer questions such as *How many?* and *When?* They do not change the meaning of a root word. A suffix has a meaning that changes the meaning of a root word.

Write a Persuasive Letter

Persuasive writing tries to change your opinion about something. With a partner, find an example of a persuasive letter. Fill in the information from the letter below:

Topic: _____

Opinion: _____

_____

Reasons for the opinion: _____

_____

Then think of a state or city rule that you would like to change. Write a letter to a public official, such as the mayor or governor. In your letter, try to persuade the official to change the rule.

- Before you write your letter, list reasons for your opinion.

- In your letter, write your main opinion in a clear sentence.

- Next, write strong reasons to support your opinion.

- Then list your reasons from most important to least important.

Quick Tip

Remember to include a heading, greeting, closing, and signature in your letter.

- Write a greeting that begins with *Dear* and the name of a public official.

- Write a closing, such as *Sincerely*.

- Include commas after the greeting and closing.

- Sign your name in the space after the closing.

Respond to the Read Aloud

The plot in a story is usually about a problem or conflict the characters are having. The solution or resolution is how the characters solve the problem.

Listen to "A Colorful Problem."

COLLABORATE

Describe the problem and the solution.

Write about the problem the kids are having and the solution they find.

Problem

↓

Steps to Solution

↓

Solution

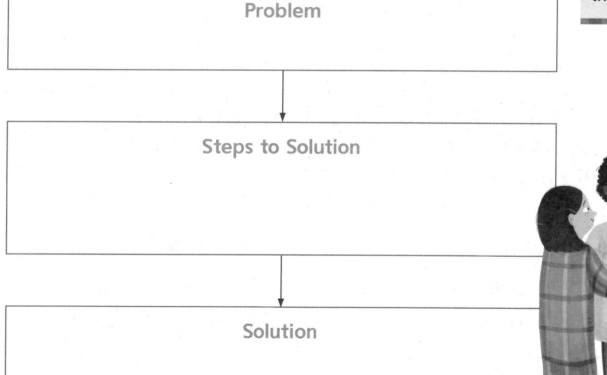

Create a Timeline

Choose one of the people shown below. Use print or online resources to create a timeline. Show four or more key events in the life of the person you choose.

Thurgood Marshall	Irma Rangel
John Hancock	Theodore Roosevelt

- Mark the years in decades.

- Write the person's date of birth on the timeline.

- Use short phrases or sentences to describe at least four important events or accomplishments in the person's life.

- Include a photo or drawing with the timeline.

Write a sentence that summarizes the information on your timeline.

_____

_____

Share the information on your timeline with a partner. Discuss the events you include in the timeline. Think about how a timeline helps readers understand a person's life.

Official portrait of the 1976 U.S. Supreme Court Justice Thurgood Marshall

Library of Congress Prints and Photographs Division ILC-JSZ62-60139I

What Did You Learn?

Use the rubric to evaluate yourself on the skills that you learned in this unit. Circle your scores below.

	excellent	good	fair	needs work
Sequence	4	3	2	1
Point of View	4	3	2	1
Author's Purpose	4	3	2	1
Timeline	4	3	2	1
Synonyms	4	3	2	1
Suffixes	4	3	2	1
Multiple-Meaning Words	4	3	2	1

What is something you want to get better at?

_____

_____

Text to Self Think about the texts you read in this unit. Tell your partner about a personal connection you made to one of the texts. Use the sentence starter to help you.

I made a connection to . . . because . . .

Present Your Work

With your partner, plan how you will present your recycling chart to the class. Use the Presenting Checklist to help you. Discuss the sentence starters below and write your answers.

An interesting fact I learned about what can be recycled is

_____

_____

_____

I would like to know more about _____

_____

_____

_____